FEB 08 2007

P9-EMK-143

LAND and WATER

Lake Huron

by Anne Ylvisaker

Consultant:
Rosanne W. Fortner, Professor of Natural Resources
and Associate Director, F. T. Stone Laboratory
The Ohio State University
School of Natural Resources
Columbus, Ohio

Capstone
press
Mankato, Minnesota

Fact Finders is published by Capstone Press,
151 Good Counsel Drive, P.O. Box 669, Mankato, Minnesota 56002.
www.capstonepress.com

Library of Congress Cataloging-in-Publication Data
Ylvisaker, Anne.
    Lake Huron / by Anne Ylvisaker.
    v. cm.—(Fact finders. Land and water)
    Includes bibliographical references (p. 31) and index.
    Contents: Lake Huron—Lake beginnings—Lake Huron's people—Trade and
industry—Pollution—Lake Huron today.
    ISBN 0-7368-2209-7 (hardcover)
    1. Huron, Lake (Mich. and Ont.)—Juvenile literature. [1. Huron, Lake (Mich. and Ont.)]
I. Title. II. Series.
F554.Y588 2004
977.4—dc21   2003000324

Editorial Credits
Erika L. Shores, editor; Juliette Peters, series designer and illustrator; Alta Schaffer,
    photo researcher; Eric Kudalis, product planning editor

Photo Credits
Cover image: Bruce Peninsula in Lake Huron, Ann & Rob Simpson

Ann & Rob Simpson, 11
Corbis, 15; Galen Rowell, 22; Tom Stewart, 23
Doranne Jacobson, 1, 20–21, 26, 27
James P. Rowan, 12–13
Macdonald Photography/Root Resources, 24–25
North Wind Picture Archives, 14, 17, 19
Photo by Carol Diehl, 6
Port Huron Museum, Port Huron, Michigan, 4–5
Visuals Unlimited/ Jakub Jasinski, 10

The Hands On activity on page 29 was adapted with permission from *Lake Erie ... Take a
Bow* by M. Canning, M. Dunlevy, and R. W. Fortner, Sea Grant Publications, Columbus,
Ohio, 1986.

Table of Contents

Chapter 1

Lake Huron

In early November 1913, the weather was unusually calm. The air was warm, and the wind was gentle.

On November 7, the weather changed. Weather systems from the Rocky Mountains, the Bering Sea, and the Caribbean Sea met over the Great Lakes. Together, the systems caused a terrible storm. Strong winds blew. Snow and ice pounded ships on Lake Huron. Waves reached 35 feet (11 meters) high. Ships were tossed around. Many ships broke apart in the icy waves.

One ship captain scratched a note on a board broken off his ship. To his wife he wrote, "Goodbye Nellie, ship

The *Charles S. Price* was one of the ships to sink on Lake Huron during the November 1913 storm.

breaking up fast. Williams." The board was later found on a New York beach.

At least eight ships sank on Lake Huron that day. More than 178 people died on the lake during the storm.

The Great Lakes

The Great Lakes of North America are Lakes Superior, Huron, Michigan, Ontario, and Erie. Straits, rivers, and canals join the Great Lakes to each other and to the Atlantic Ocean.

Lake Huron lies between Canada and the United States. Ontario, Canada, and Michigan border Lake Huron.

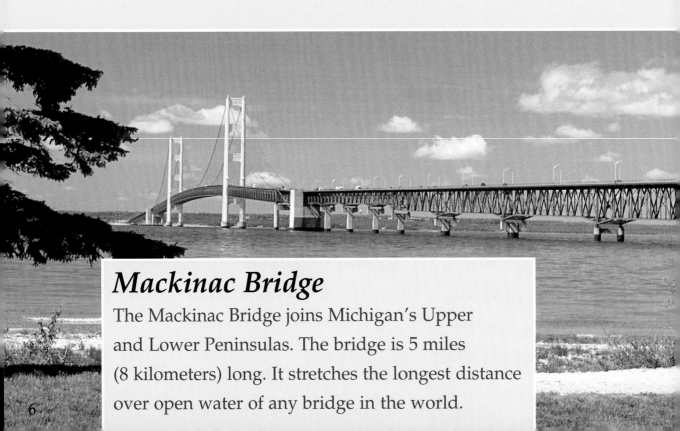

Mackinac Bridge

The Mackinac Bridge joins Michigan's Upper and Lower Peninsulas. The bridge is 5 miles (8 kilometers) long. It stretches the longest distance over open water of any bridge in the world.

Lake Huron lies between Canada and the United States.

Lake Huron is the fifth largest lake in the world. It is the second largest Great Lake. Huron is 206 miles (332 kilometers) long and 183 miles (295 kilometers) wide. The lake's average depth is 195 feet (59 meters). In some areas, Lake Huron reaches 750 feet (229 meters) deep.

Chapter 2

Lake Beginnings

Thousands of years ago, glaciers covered the Great Lakes area. These slow-moving sheets of ice were more than 1 mile (2 kilometers) thick. The glaciers' weight pressed down the land. Glaciers carved out wide valleys. Water filled the valleys when the glaciers melted. The Great Lakes formed.

Glaciers shaped Lake Huron's shores. Lake Huron's northern shore is part of the Canadian Shield. The Canadian Shield is a rocky area that was once a mountain range. Sandy beaches and thick forests cover the other areas around Lake Huron.

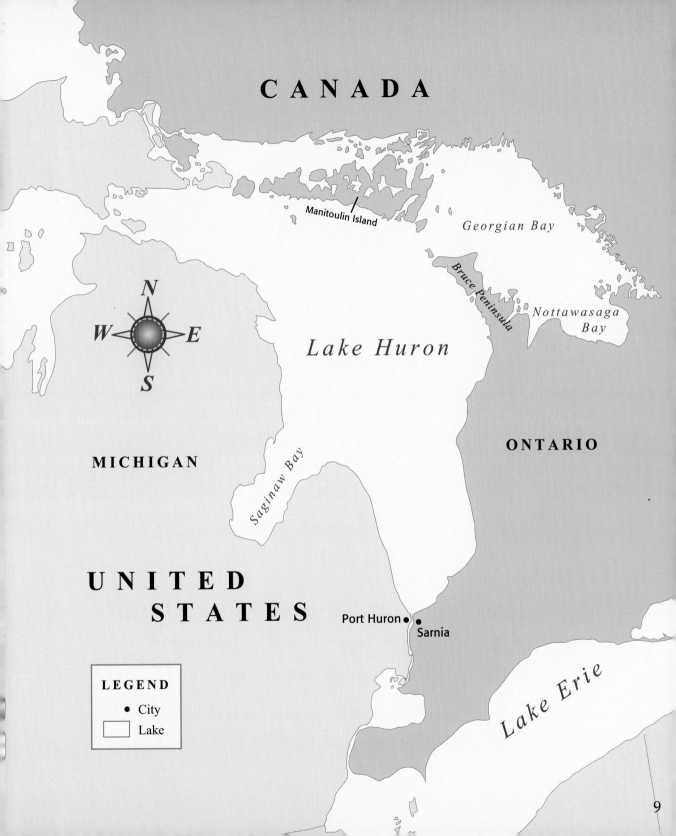

CANADA

Manitoulin Island

Georgian Bay

Bruce Peninsula

Nottawasaga Bay

Lake Huron

ONTARIO

MICHIGAN

Saginaw Bay

UNITED STATES

Port Huron •

• Sarnia

Lake Erie

N
W E
S

LEGEND

• City

☐ Lake

Forests grow along
Lake Huron's shores.

Islands

Lake Huron has more islands than the other Great Lakes.
Manitoulin Island is Lake Huron's largest island.
Along with the Bruce Peninsula, Manitoulin Island
separates the lake from Georgian Bay. Georgian Bay
is so large it is sometimes called the sixth Great Lake.

Manitoulin Island

Manitoulin Island is the largest freshwater island in the world. It covers 1,067 square miles (2,764 square kilometers). Manitoulin Island is part of Ontario, Canada. Six Ojibwa Indian reserves are located on the island. Reserves are areas of land set aside by the Canadian government for native people.

Chapter 3

Lake Huron's People

People living in North America moved north as the glaciers melted. By the 1600s, Huron Indians lived in the area around Georgian Bay. They built log walls around their villages. Men cut down forests to make farmland. Women planted fields and took care of crops. Men hunted deer. Women used the deerskins to make clothing.

Early Explorers

Early European explorers in North America wanted to find a water route to Asia. In the 1600s, French explorers

Huron Indians built homes called longhouses.

Samuel de Champlain
first explored Lake Huron.

thought they had found the passage. Instead,
they had discovered the Great Lakes.

French explorer Samuel de Champlain came
to Lake Huron in the early 1600s. He wrote
about the beavers he saw. French fur traders came
to the area. They traded with the Huron Indians
for beaver furs. Explorers like Champlain made a
great deal of money selling the furs in Europe.
Europeans used them for clothing and hats.

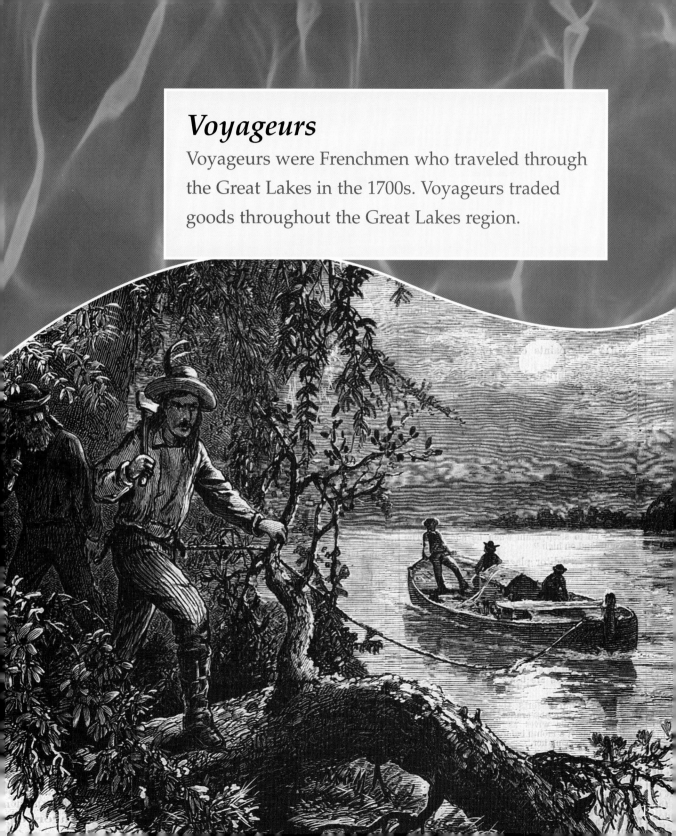

Voyageurs

Voyageurs were Frenchmen who traveled through the Great Lakes in the 1700s. Voyageurs traded goods throughout the Great Lakes region.

Chapter 4

Trade and Industry

When Europeans came, the Huron Indians' lives changed. The Indians were able to trade animal skins for tools and cookware. Europeans wanted to bring Christianity to the Huron. Champlain sent priests from France to Lake Huron. In 1639, the mission St. Marie-among-the-Hurons became the first European settlement in the area.

The Iroquois Indians became angry that the French were trading with the Huron. The Iroquois tried to stop trade between the Huron and the French. The Iroquois fought with the Huron and French. The Iroquois forced them out of the area.

The Iroquois Indians fought with French explorers and the Huron Indians.

The Iroquois killed many priests and burned the mission. No one settled in that region again for 200 years. Instead, missionaries set up missions in other areas around Lake Huron.

Fur Trade, Logging, and Minerals

The Straits of Mackinac were the center of the Lake Huron fur trade. The French set up forts to protect their claim to the area. Both the French and the American Indians trapped beavers. Soon, people from Great Britain wanted to join the fur trade. After much fighting, the British won control of the area.

Americans also wanted control of the fur trade. After the War of 1812 (1812–1814), the area became part of the United States. Americans made a lot of money by selling furs in Europe. By 1842, most of the beavers had been killed. People could no longer make money trading furs.

Soon, lumber and mining industries started near Lake Huron. Loggers cut

down trees to make paper and build homes
and businesses. In the 1800s, people discovered
minerals on the northern shore of Lake Huron.
Gold, iron, copper, and zinc were taken from
the ground there.

The Straits of Mackinac let ships
travel between the Great Lakes.

Chapter 5

Pollution

Lake Huron is the quietest of the Great Lakes. Few towns and factories surround the lake. These factors help keep the lake cleaner than the other Great Lakes. But pollution from nearby farms has harmed Lake Huron's water and wildlife.

Farmers around the area need to protect their crops from insects. For many years, farmers sprayed DDT and other chemicals on the crops to kill insects. Rain then washed the chemicals into rivers. The rivers carried the chemicals into Lake Huron. The chemicals got into the lake's fish. Eating these fish harmed animals and people.

Many farms are near Lake Huron. Farmers must be careful not to pollute the lake.

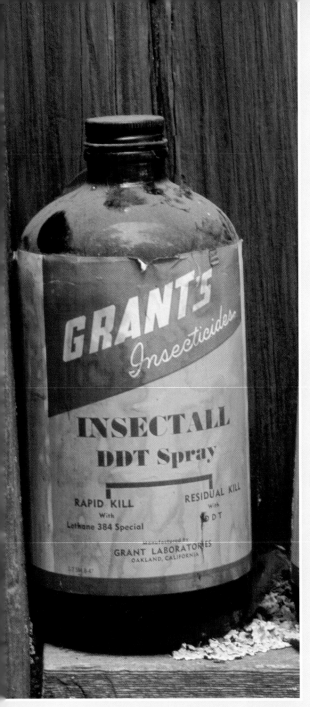

Before the 1970s, farmers used DDT on their crops.

People living near Lake Huron wanted to protect the lake. In 1972, the U.S. and Canadian governments made it against the law to use dangerous chemicals on crops. But some harmful chemicals can still be found in the water. Today, more than 40 groups along Lake Huron's shores work to keep the lake healthy. These groups teach people about ways to keep Lake Huron clean.

People living near Lake Huron work to keep the areas around the lake clean.

23

Chapter 6

Lake Huron Today

Today, people use Lake Huron for many different activities. Lake Huron's location as part of the St. Lawrence Seaway makes it important to shipping. Ships travel through Lake Huron to bring goods from Lake Superior to the other Great Lakes or the Atlantic Ocean.

Sarnia, Ontario, and Port Huron, Michigan, are the two biggest cities on the lake. A large amount of Ontario's oil is shipped through the port at Sarnia. Port Huron is home to businesses related to the car industry.

Grain is loaded onto ships at ports on Lake Huron.

Tourism

Many people enjoy visiting Lake Huron. Visitors to Lake Huron's beaches enjoy swimming and boating. Other people fish.

Lake Huron's islands and strong storms have caused many shipwrecks. Lake Huron's water is very clear and cold. The sunken ships do not rot easily. Today, tourists go scuba

People visit Lake Huron's beaches in summer.

diving or look through glass-bottom boats to see these sunken ships. Popular places to see sunken ships are in Fathom Five Provincial Park or other areas in Georgian Bay.

The beauty of Lake Huron and its nearby areas attract many visitors each year. People living near Lake Huron work to protect the lake. They want people to enjoy Lake Huron in the future.

Visitors to Tobermory, Ontario, view the Big Tub lighthouse. The lighthouse shines light into the Big Tub harbor of Lake Huron.

Fast Facts

Length: 206 miles (332 kilometers)

Width: 183 miles (295 kilometers)

Average depth: 195 feet (59 meters)

Maximum depth: 750 feet (229 meters)

Shoreline length: 3,830 miles (6,164 kilometers)

Population surrounding the lake: 3 million

Exploration: Lake Huron was the first Great Lake explored by Europeans.

Fish: Many kinds of fish live in Lake Huron. These fish include smallmouth bass, lake herring, northern pike, bowfin, and pumpkinseed.

Hands On: Study the Great Lakes

People use maps to learn more about places. You can learn more about the Great Lakes with this activity.

What You Need

Map of Great Lakes on page 7
Paper
Pencil

What You Do

1. Write down which Great Lake is the largest.
2. Which lake is the smallest?
3. Use the compass on the map to decide which direction you would travel from Lake Superior to Lake Ontario.
4. If you were traveling from Ohio, in which direction would you go to reach Lake Huron?
5. Write down which lakes border the state of Michigan.
6. Write down the names of the state and the province bordering Lake Huron.
7. Write down the names of the cities you might visit if you traveled on Lake Huron through Lake Erie and into Lake Ontario.

Glossary

glacier (GLAY-shur)—a large, slow-moving sheet of ice and snow

industry (IN-duh-stree)—businesses that make products or provide services

mission (MISH-uhn)—a church or place that is built to teach people about Christian religions

port (PORT)—a harbor or place where boats and ships can dock or anchor safely

priest (PREEST)—a member of a church who leads church services and performs religious rites

strait (STRAYT)—a narrow strip of water that connects two larger bodies of water

Internet Sites

Do you want to find out more about Lake Huron?
Let FactHound, our fact-finding hound dog, do the research for you.

Here's how:
1) Visit *http://www.facthound.com*
2) Type in the **Book ID** number: **0736822097**
3) Click on **FETCH IT.**

FactHound will fetch Internet sites picked by our editors just for you!

Read More

Beckett, Harry. *Lake Huron.* Great Lakes of North America. Vero Beach, Fla.: Rourke, 1999.

Koestler-Grack, Rachel A. *The Iroquois: Longhouse Builders.* America's First Peoples. Mankato, Minn.: Blue Earth Books, 2003.

Smithyman, Kathryn, and Bobbie Kalman. *Nations of the Western Great Lakes.* Native Nations of North America. New York: Crabtree, 2003.

Index